Grades K-1

Art Projects That Dazzle & Delight

BY KAREN BACKUS, LINDA EVANS, MARY THOMPSON, AND KAREN TRUSH

SCHOLASTIC
PROFESSIONAL BOOKS

NEW YORK • TORONTO • LONDON • AUCKLAND • SYDNEY
MEXICO CITY • NEW DELHI • HONG KONG • BUENOS AIRES

This book is dedicated to all those "children at heart"

who have inspired us to teach.

Thank you,

Karen Backus, Linda Evans,

Mary Thompson, and Karen Trush

Front cover and interior design by Kathy Massaro
Interior illustrations by James Graham Hale

ISBN: 0-439-15387-5

Contents

Introduction

This book grew from a workshop titled Fabulous Projects for Elementary Art, which we presented in 1998 at the New York State Art Teachers Conference in Albany, New York. Using ideas from our presentation, as well as many from our current classes, we have compiled workable and easy-to-manage art activities that will enhance your classroom and help children develop an appreciation for the arts.

The lessons follow a step-by-step format and help children focus on the building blocks of art concepts and vocabulary. The projects include a wide variety of techniques and materials. Using both imagination and creativity, the possibilities are endless. We hope you will enjoy sharing these hands-on activities with your class.

Helpful Hints

Preparation

- A few steps of preparation can prevent disasters. In advance, plan the cleanup procedure for each project. Children love to help, and with a little direction, you'll have a quick and effective cleanup.

- In advance, gather supplies and cut paper to the size specified for each activity. (The paper size does not need to be exact.)

- Always try an art project yourself before presenting it to children. Your experience will serve you well in anticipating any problems that might arise.

- When children are going to cut something along the fold of a folded piece of paper, have them first mark the folded edge with an *X*. When it's time to cut, tell children to "hold the fold."

To save time, paper, and erasers, first have children practice drawing a shape with a finger on paper or in the air. This step lets you check for understanding and offer help in working out potential problems.

Paint smocks are the best insurance for hassle-free painting. Men's short-sleeved T-shirts or button-down shirts worn backward offer great coverage.

If the artwork needs to dry, plan ahead for a place to put it. A clothesline and clothespins may work where space is limited.

If children are easily distracted or are eager to begin and don't wait for directions, distribute the art supplies on an "as needed" basis.

If a project calls for a certain mood, plan to play music that is related to the activity.

Before children begin a project, have them write their names on the back of their paper.

Introducing a Project

Whenever possible, show students photographs, drawings, or other visuals that relate to each project. For example, display landscape photographs or paintings to introduce Torn-Paper Landscapes (pages 11–13) and real flowers or photographs of flowers to introduce Blooming Beauties (pages 27–29). Suggestions are presented throughout the book.

Introduce children to artistic terms that may be unfamiliar to them. For each activity, you'll find a short list of words that will be helpful for children to know as they engage in the activity. These words are highlighted the first time they appear in the activity.

In the sections entitled Let's Begin, you'll find suggested ways to introduce each project.

Drawing

Many lessons in this book refer to the "look and draw" technique. This is a step-by-step method of drawing that works well with young children. The object is not to have the children's art be a copy of yours but rather to help them succeed in executing the activities. This method is especially useful in assisting children in positioning objects in particular places on their paper.

When using this method, position yourself in a spot that allows the class a clear view. Draw a few lines at a time, have children observe, and then have them follow your example. Keep in mind that the beauty of children's artwork lies in their unique way of seeing the world. Look for ways to encourage their originality and to help them express their ideas.

Encourage children always to try! Sharing your own struggles may make some children feel more at ease when attempting something new.

Painting

Put tempera paints on foam trays or paper plates for easy cleanup.

Use garbage bags to cover work surfaces. Cut off the bottom of a bag and slit one side, then tape it to the sides of a table. You can wipe off the garbage bag cover and reuse it if desired.

To clean tempera paint off paintbrushes, soak for ten minutes in water with a little dishwashing soap. The paint will rinse off quickly.

Displaying Children's Work

How artwork is displayed can make the difference between "so-so" and "wow!" viewer responses. You'll find specific suggestions for displaying each of the projects in this book. Try out your own ideas, and encourage students to contribute theirs as well.

A simple way to mount artwork starts with a little planning. For a painting activity, give students paper that has been trimmed an inch on each side. For example, cut a 12- by 18-inch sheet of paper so that it's 11 inches by 17 inches. You can then glue the painting onto the larger sheet to create a border.

Use large background paper to unify your displays and help avoid the distraction of wall color or patterns.

Watercolor Buildings

Children use watercolors and crayons to create a collaborative class mural of different types of buildings.

Materials

- pictures of different types of buildings
- 12- by 18-inch heavy white paper
- black crayons
- watercolor paints
- paintbrushes
- water containers
- scissors
- glue
- large sheet of craft paper (the size of a classroom bulletin board)

New Art Words

architecture

geometric shapes

horizontal

vertical

overlap

mural

 Let's Begin

Display the photographs and discuss different types of buildings. Introduce the term **architecture**. Invite children to describe the exterior of their homes as well as the buildings where their parents and other family members work. Talk about the shapes of buildings as well as the shapes of windows and roofs. Help children relate these shapes to **geometric shapes** such as rectangles, squares, triangles, and circles. Explain to children that they will each illustrate a building using different shapes and then put the buildings together to make a community. Encourage children to choose different kinds of buildings for their community.

Pass out the materials. Then demonstrate the following procedures as children follow along.

Step by Step

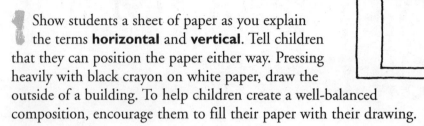

1 Show students a sheet of paper as you explain the terms **horizontal** and **vertical**. Tell children that they can position the paper either way. Pressing heavily with black crayon on white paper, draw the outside of a building. To help children create a well-balanced composition, encourage them to fill their paper with their drawing.

2 Continuing to press hard with the black crayon, add details such as windows, doors, flower boxes, curtains, chimneys, siding, and signs.

3 When the drawings are complete, apply watercolor paint over the buildings. A thin application of paint will allow the crayon to show through. Let the paint dry.

4 To create a community, help children cut out the buildings and mount them on craft paper. Demonstrate how to **overlap** buildings to create depth.

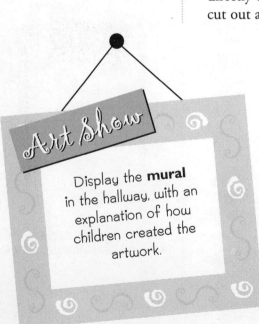

One Step More

Children may wish to add details such as trees, flowers, birds, and street signs to the community. They can do this by using markers or crayons directly on the background paper, or by making individual drawings to cut out and paste onto the paper.

Art Show

Display the **mural** in the hallway, with an explanation of how children created the artwork.

Bookshelf

All in a Day by Mitsumasa Anno and Raymond Briggs (Philomel Books, 1986)

A House Is a House for Me by Mary Ann Hoberman (Viking Press, 1978)

Houses by Claude Delafosse and Gallimard Jeunesse (Scholastic, 1998)

The Little House by Virginia Lee Burton (Houghton Mifflin, 1978)

Shaping Houses

Children learn about different styles of homes from around the world and, using simple paper shapes, create collage houses.

Materials

- pictures of various houses from around the world
- 12- by 18-inch white construction paper
- 9- by 9-inch paper squares (various colors)
- 1 1/2- by 2-inch paper rectangles (various colors, can include some larger and smaller rectangles as well)
- paper triangles with one 10-inch side (various colors)
- glue
- crayons
- fine-tipped markers
- yarn
- fabric scraps
- scissors

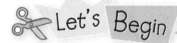 Let's Begin

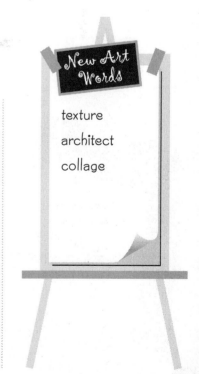

New Art Words

texture

architect

collage

Display photographs of different kinds of homes from around the world: apartment buildings, colonial and modern houses, townhouses, mobile homes, as well as more unusual homes such as castles, igloos, and Iroquois longhouses. Discuss the different materials used to build these homes—for example, wood, brick, aluminum, shingles, and stone. Introduce the new words children will learn in this activity: **texture** describes the way a surface feels, such as smooth or rough; an **architect** is a person who designs buildings; a **collage** is a picture made from different materials that have been assembled and glued together.

Pass out the materials. Then demonstrate the following procedures as children follow along.

Step by Step

1 Ask children to imagine that they are
architects who have been asked to design a
house using simple shapes. Review the shapes
that children will use. Start with a square.
Then ask: "If the building is a square, what shape might the roof be?"
Place a square and triangle on a sheet of white paper and glue into place.
Glue rectangles to add windows and doors. Encourage children to use
the shapes that best fit the kind of home they wish to build.

2 Have children use crayons or markers to
draw the textures of different materials
such as brick, wood, or shingles.

3 Tell children to draw themselves inside
the house looking out a window.
Children can glue on yarn for hair and fabric
for clothing or curtains.

4 Children may also wish to personalize
their houses by drawing flowers, trees, a sidewalk, a dog, a swing in
the yard, or a cat in the window.

One Step More

Children often have a story to tell about their pictures. Set aside a time
for children to share these visual stories.

Bookshelf

Homes and Houses Long Ago by Helen Edom
(Usbourne, 1989)

Houses and Homes by Ann Morris
(Lothrop, Lee & Shepard, 1992)

How a House Is Built by Gail Gibbons
(Holiday House, 1990)

The Napping House by Audrey Wood
(Harcourt Brace Jovanovich, 1984)

Art Show

Stretch a string from
one wall to another.
To create a classroom
street, hang the house
collages on the string.

Torn-Paper Landscapes

Children create countryside scenes from torn construction paper and learn how distance affects size and color.

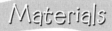
Materials

- examples of landscape paintings or photographs of landscapes
- 9- by 12-inch blue paper
- 4- by 12-inch strips of various shades of green paper
- glue
- markers or crayons
- 10- by 13-inch brown paper (optional, for mounting)

New Art Words

landscape
foreground
background
middle ground
overlapping

Let's Begin

Display photographs or paintings of **landscapes** (natural scenes). Help children look for the different colors within a picture. Point out that colors are usually brighter in the **foreground** (up close), whereas colors fade in the distant **background** (far away). Ask children to describe how objects appear in the foreground (larger) and in the background (smaller). Explain that the **middle ground** is the space in between.

   Pass out the materials. Then demonstrate the following procedures as children follow along.

Step by Step

1 Explain to children that they will create a landscape, using torn colored paper. Begin with the blue paper, which will serve as both the base of the project and the sky.

2 Have children select the darkest green paper strip. Demonstrate how to hold the paper flat on a tabletop in a vertical position. Place one hand on the paper and slowly pull a tear toward yourself. Tear about an inch off along the length of the strip. Glue this piece approximately two inches from the top of the blue paper to create the background color. Tell children that an uneven tear will make a more interesting landscape.

3 Next, have children take a medium-color green strip and tear another uneven line. Explain that this strip will represent the middle ground. Model how to place the second strip so that it is **overlapping** the first. Then glue the second strip in place. It is impossible to make a mistake, because any torn piece can be layered and glued onto the landscape.

4 Show children how to complete the foreground with a strip of the lightest green paper. Tear an uneven line along the length of the strip and place it at the bottom of the composition. Glue the strip in place and let it dry.

5 Using crayon or marker, illustrate trees in several different sizes. In
the foreground, draw large trees. Draw medium-sized trees in the
middle ground and small trees in the background. You can relate the
tree sizes to the story of the three bears:
Papa, Mama, and Baby. Have children
complete their landscapes by adding trees.
You might also show children how to draw a
road that is wide in the foreground and
narrows as it moves into the distance.

One Step More

Invite children to repeat this activity, experimenting with different-
colored strips to create the foreground, middle ground, and background.
Talk about the colors that work best for each part of the landscape. The
colors do not need to be realistic.

Bookshelf

All the Places to Love by Patricia MacLachlan
    (HarperCollins, 1994)

Letting Swift River Go by Jane Yolen
    (Little, Brown and Company, 1992)

Places in Art by Anthea Peppin
    (Millbrook Press, 1992)

Sun Song by Jean Marzollo (HarperCollins, 1995)

Window by Jeannie Baker (Greenwillow Books, 1991)

Art Show

To create a mock frame,
mount the landscapes on
brown paper. Then create
a wood-grained effect
by drawing lines with
marker on the frame.

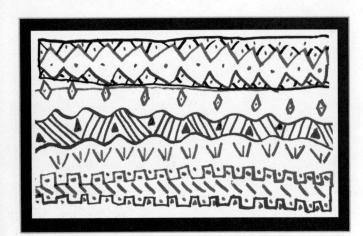

Line Dancing

Children create intricate designs in a project that combines art and math skills.

Materials

- examples of various patterns
  (on fabric, wrapping paper, and so on)
- cassette tapes of rhythmic music
  (such as jazz, new age, and percussion)
- broad-tipped markers
- 10- by 16-inch white drawing paper
- 12- by 18-inch colored paper (for mounting)
- glue

New Art Words

pattern

line

rhythm

horizontal

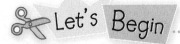 Let's Begin

Read aloud one of the books listed under Bookshelf to initiate a discussion of line patterns. Show children examples of various patterns and then have them look for patterns on their clothing and around the classroom. Explain that one kind of **pattern** is a **line** that repeats over and over, and that a pattern may have more than one line in its design. Point out that lines have **rhythm**, just as music does. Illustrate this by playing music with clearly defined rhythms.

Pass out the materials and demonstrate the following procedures. As children work on their projects, play different types of music to inspire repetition and patterns.

Step by Step

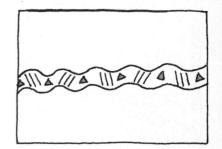

1 Discuss the term **horizontal**, and explain that all the patterns children draw for this project will be horizontal. With a marker, draw a wavy horizontal line across the center of a sheet of white paper.

2 Choose a different color and add details to the first line, repeating across the paper.

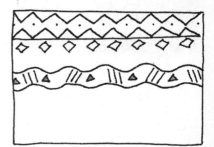

3 Begin a new pattern about 1 1/2 inches above the first pattern. (Show children how 1 1/2 inches can be approximately measured by holding three fingers together.)

4 Add details to the pattern, using new colors. (Usually three or four colors are adequate for each new pattern.)

5 Continue to fill the paper by adding new patterns above and below the first.

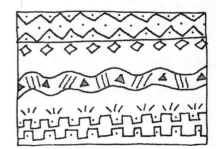

6 Help children mount their completed projects by gluing them onto the colored paper.

One Step More

After the project has been completed, teach children a simple line dance to further illustrate the concept of repeating patterns.

Bookshelf

Hide and Snake by Keith Barker
    (Harcourt Brace Jovanovich, 1991)
Lines by Philip Yenawine (Delacorte Press, 1991)
Straight Is a Line by Sharon Lerner
    (Lerner Publications, 1991)
Ten Little Rabbits by Virginia Grossman
    (Chronicle Books, 1991)

Art Show

Display children's work along with samples of patterned clothing or fabric or pictures of patterns in nature.

Mitten Kittens

Children create adorable kittens peeking from the tops of patterned mittens.

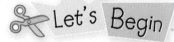

Materials

- mitten template (page 18)
- kitten-face template (page 19)
- 9- by 12-inch white or light-colored drawing paper
- pencils
- markers
- scissors
- crayons
- glue

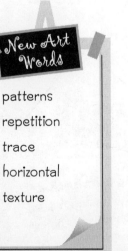

New Art Words

patterns

repetition

trace

horizontal

texture

✂ Let's Begin

Read aloud the nursery rhyme "The Three Little Kittens" to introduce the theme of kittens and mittens. Point out that many mittens have colorful **patterns** on them. Have children find patterns on their clothing. Discuss the **repetition** in the designs. Point out that some of the words in "The Three Little Kittens" also repeat.

In advance, cut out enough mitten and kitten templates for children to share. Pass out the materials and demonstrate the following procedures.

Step by Step

Trace the mitten template onto the drawing paper.

2 Position the mitten so the opening is at the top. Use markers to draw **horizontal** designs on the mitten. More than one color may be used to create each pattern. Encourage children to use shapes, numbers, and letters in their patterns.

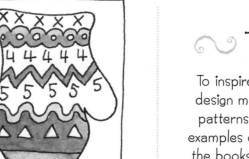

3 Cut out the mitten.

4 Trace the kitten-face template onto another sheet of paper and cut it out.

5 Use markers to add facial features. Crayons can be used to draw the whiskers and create the **texture** of fur.

6 Put a small amount of glue on the front of the mitten along the top. Glue the kitten to the mitten.

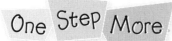

Sing or dance with children to "The Three Little Kittens" song.

Tip

To inspire children to design more complex patterns, show them examples of patterns in the books listed under Bookshelf.

 **Bookshelf**

Mother Goose Remembers by Clare Beaton (Barefoot Books, 2000)

The Cat by Giovanna Mantegazza (St. Martin's Press, 1992)

Hide and Snake by Keith Barker (Harcourt Brace Jovanovich, 1991)

Hot Air Henry by Mary Calhoun (W. Morrow, 1981)

The Kids' Cat Book by Tomie DePaola (Holiday House, 1979)

Lines by Philip Yenawine (Delacorte Press, 1991)

Art Show

String a clothesline across the room and clip the Mitten Kittens onto it with clothespins.

Mitten Template

Art Projects That Dazzle & Delight: Grades K–1   Scholastic Professional Books

Kitten Template

Colorful Clowns

Children learn about body proportions as they create colorful clowns.

Materials

- clown toys or pictures of clowns
- 12- by 18-inch white drawing paper
- fine-tipped markers
- crayons
- scissors
- glue
- 18- by 24-inch colored construction paper

New Art Words

solid

primary colors

secondary colors

overlapping

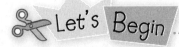

Let's Begin

Using a volunteer or a clown doll as a model, have children observe that arms are attached to shoulders, legs are attached to hips, and the head is attached to the neck. Explain that the main part of the body is called the trunk. Discuss body proportions.

Pass out the materials and demonstrate the following procedures. Model the steps for children as they follow along.

Step by Step

1 Use a marker on a sheet of white paper to draw a head about the size of a baseball. (Using markers instead of pencils encourages children to spend less time erasing.) Tell children to begin with any color they prefer.

2 Use the look-and-draw technique (you draw as children look, then children draw) to outline the rest of the clown. Add arms, beginning at the shoulders. Add a body, hands, and legs.

3 Discuss the different types of clown faces. Some clowns appear sad and lonely. Others, such as whiteface clowns, wear elegant makeup. Auguste clowns wear extravagant makeup and baggy suits. Draw a clown face with exaggerated features. Add curly hair, a hat, and big shoes. Show children how to exaggerate these for a humorous effect. Draw a bow tie or ruffle.

4 Using different-colored markers, draw patterns and line designs on the clown's suit.

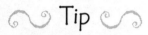
5 Color the drawing with crayons. As you do so, explain the concept of **solid**.

6 On another sheet of paper, draw three balloons that are each about the size of a baseball. Color the balloons with **primary colors** (red, blue, and yellow). Cut out the balloons.

7 Mount the clowns on colored construction paper, offset to the left bottom corner of the colored paper. Glue the balloons in the top right corner so they are **overlapping**. Draw balloon strings from the balloons to the clown's closest hand.

Tip

Introduce the concept of mixing colors by overlapping the balloon circles. Then color the overlapped section with **secondary colors** (orange between red and yellow, green between blue and yellow, purple between red and blue).

One Step More

An interesting fact to tell children about clown makeup is that each clown has his or her personal face and always puts on the same face for a performance. A clown never copies another clown's face, unless a clown retires and gives his or her face design to another clown to use.

Art Show

Draw a circus ring on a large sheet of brown or white craft paper. Display the clowns in and around the ring.

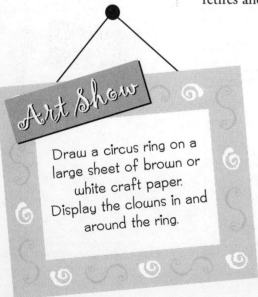

Bookshelf

Clown by Quentin Blake (H. Holt, 1996)

The Clown-Arounds Go on Vacation by Joanna Cole (Parents Magazine Press, 1983)

The Clown-Arounds Have a Party by Joanna Cole (Parents Magazine Press, 1982)

Clowning Around by Cathryn Falwell (Orchard Books, 1991)

Parts by Tedd Arnold (Dial Books, 1997)

Teddy's Patterned Shirt

Children enhance their math skills as they create patterns and geometric shapes on a colorful shirt for a teddy bear.

Materials

- shirt template (page 26)
- circle template (page 26)
- 9- by 12-inch white or light-colored drawing paper
- pencils
- scissors
- markers
- 12- by 18-inch brown paper
- glue

New Art Word

patterns

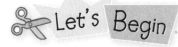 Let's Begin

Ask children to observe their classmates' clothing. Look for **patterns** with colorful images. Tell children that they will be using repeat patterns to design a shirt for a teddy bear friend.

In advance, copy and cut out enough shirt and circle templates for children to share. Then pass out the materials and demonstrate the following procedures as children follow along.

Step by Step

1 Use a pencil to trace the shirt template onto white or light-colored paper. Then cut it out.

2 Using markers, demonstrate how to make a simple geometric pattern. (Show children the patterns below.) Allow children to copy or create patterns of their choice on the teddy bear shirts.

3 Position the brown paper vertically, and glue the shirt in the center of the paper.

4 Use the look-and-draw method to draw the bear's body parts. Place the circle template above the shirt. Trace the template to create a large snout. Inside the circle, draw a nose and a mouth that curls into a smile. Draw the head around the nose. Draw two circles for eyes and two ears. Add four paws.

5 Cut out the finished bears.

Tip

To use the look-and-draw method, you draw as children observe. Then children draw what you drew in their own unique styles. In this project, each child's teddy bear will take on its own personality.

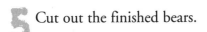 One Step More

Children might use their bears to act out a favorite teddy bear story.

 Bookshelf

Brown Bear Brown Bear, What Do You See?
by Bill Martin, Jr. (Holt, Rinehart and Winston, 1967)

Moonbear by Frank Asch (Little Simon, 1993)

Ragged Bear by Brigitte Weninger
(North-South Books, 1996)

Art Show

Mount the bears on a large sheet of paper and then invite families to a classroom Teddy Bear Picnic!

Circle and Shirt
Templates

Art Projects That Dazzle & Delight: Grades K–1   Scholastic Professional Books

Blooming Beauties

Using Georgia O'Keeffe's artwork as a model, children learn that artists often see things in a unique way. In this project children create a "garden" of flower paintings.

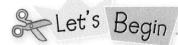 ## Materials

- flowers or photographs of flowers
- examples of Georgia O'Keeffe's flower paintings
- 11- by 11-inch white drawing paper
- pencils
- black crayons
- tempera paint
- paintbrushes
- water containers
- scissors
- glue
- 12- by 12-inch colored construction paper
- 4- by 4-inch yellow construction paper

New Art Words

enlarged
focal point

✂ Let's Begin

Display a bouquet of flowers or photographs of flowers. Draw children's attention to the different petal shapes and colors. Then show children examples of flowers painted by Georgia O'Keeffe. Help children make comparisons between the real flowers and those in the paintings. Discuss the way O'Keeffe "sees" the flowers she paints (the flowers are **enlarged**, with the center as the **focal point**).

Pass out the materials. Then demonstrate the following procedures as children follow along.

Step by Step

1 Use the look-and-draw process for each step of this project. With pencil, draw a circle in the center of a sheet of white paper. The circle should be about the size of a tennis ball.

2 Demonstrate how to draw a curved line from the circle to the upper corner of the paper. This line should droop down.

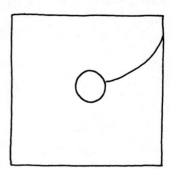

3 To complete the petal, draw a second curved line from the center. This line should curve up.

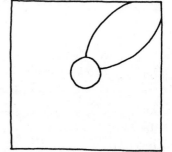

4 Draw three more petals, one in each corner of the page.

5 Follow the same procedure to make four smaller petals in between the first four. Then add smaller petals around the center of the flower.

6 Show children how to trace around the flower outline with a black crayon.

7 Choose three colors of paint. Paint the center of the flower one color, the smaller petals a second color, and the large petals a third color. Encourage children to add details such as shaded areas on the petals or pistils and stamens in the center. When the paint has dried, cut out the flower and glue it onto a sheet of colored paper.

8 Using black crayon on yellow paper, draw a bumblebee by making an oval about the size of an egg. Draw a smaller circle for the head, curved lines for the wings, and a small triangle for the tail. Create details such as stripes and eyes.

9 Cut out the bumblebee and glue it onto the flower.

One Step More

Introduce and compare flower paintings by other famous artists such as Vincent Van Gogh, Claude Monet, or Paul Cézanne. Talk about their different styles and techniques.

Bookshelf

Alison's Zinnia by Anita Lobel
(Greenwillow Books, 1990)

Planting a Rainbow by Lois Ehlert
(Harcourt Brace Jovanovich, 1988)

Rosy's Garden: A Child's Keepsake of Flowers
by Elizabeth Laird (Philomel Books, 1990)

Usborne First Nature Flowers by Rosamund
Kidman Cox and Barbara Cork (Usborne, 1990)

Art Show

To make a garden display, hang the flower paintings on black paper. Tuck a few oversized paper leaves behind the paintings.

Plant Pictures

**Children develop
observational skills as they
draw a potted plant.**

Materials

- potted plant (spider or snake plants work well)
- 10- by 16-inch white drawing paper
- pencils
- black markers
- crayons (various shades of yellow, blue, and green)

New Art Words

overlapping
foreground
background

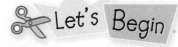 Let's Begin

Display a green plant and have children observe the layers of leaves. You might describe the **overlapping** leaves as "one arm on top of the other." Point out that part of the bottom arm is hidden. To help children understand spatial relationships, have them look at the plant and locate the **foreground**, or the area that is closest to the viewer, and the **background**, or the area that is farthest away.

   Pass out the materials. Then demonstrate the following procedures as children follow along.

Step by Step

1 Draw two slightly curved "smile" lines for the top and base of the plant container. Connect the top and bottom curves with two lines. (You may choose to draw with marker, or draw in pencil and go over the lines later with marker.)

2 After closely observing the plant, draw a leaf in the **foreground**. Start at the top of the container and draw a curved line in the shape of the leaf. When you reach the tip of the leaf, draw a line that connects back to the plant container. Explain that the shape looks like the top of a banana.

3 Next, draw a leaf in the **background**. Begin with a curved line, stopping when the line reaches the first leaf. Jump over the leaf and continue to complete the end of the leaf on the other side. Continue adding leaves without drawing on top of other leaves.

4 Notice the patterns created by the veins on each leaf. Using crayon, draw these patterns on the leaves. To create an interesting effect, blend colors together by rubbing over them with the side of an unwrapped crayon. Select yellow crayons to highlight the tops of the leaves. Use blue crayons on the bottom edge of a leaf to create a shadow. Layer blue and yellow to form shades of green.

5 Have children decorate their pots with patterns or solid colors.

One Step More

Show examples of the work of artist Henri Rousseau, who used plants from French gardens to inspire his jungle paintings.

Bookshelf

Cornelius: A Fable by Leo Lionni (Pantheon Books, 1983)

The Great Kapok Tree: A Tale of the Amazon Rain Forest by Lynne Cherry (Harcourt Brace Jovanovich, 1990)

Art Show

Display children's drawings along with the plant that they drew and an explanation of the process.

The Best Bouquet

Children use paper towel rolls to print an arrangement of flowers under a rainbow.

Materials

- pictures of rainbows
- paper towel rolls
- scissors
- crayons
- 8- by 11-inch heavy white paper
- paintbrushes (various sizes)
- tempera paint (blue, green, and other colors)
- water containers
- paper plates
- 9- by 12-inch black or colored construction paper (optional, for mounting)

New Art Words

printmaking

series

composition

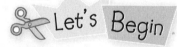

Let's Begin

Discuss the colors of the rainbow and the order in which the colors appear (red, orange, yellow, green, blue, indigo, and violet). Show children pictures of rainbows and ask them to identify the colors.

In advance, prepare five or six paper towel rolls to use for printing flowers. On one end of the roll, cut one-inch slits approximately one inch apart. Make five slits and fold the cardboard to create five flower petals.

Pass out the materials. Then demonstrate the following procedures as children follow along.

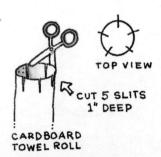

TOP VIEW

CUT 5 SLITS 1" DEEP

CARDBOARD TOWEL ROLL

FOLD BACK FLAPS

Step by Step

1 Position a sheet of white paper vertically. Starting with red crayon at the top of the paper, draw a curved band about one inch thick from one edge of the paper to the other. Explain that this is the beginning of the rainbow. Repeat the procedure with orange, yellow, green, blue, and violet crayons. Make sure each color band touches the next.

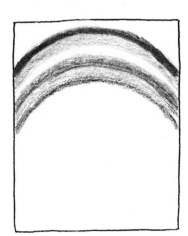

2 Paint the entire remaining surface of the paper with watered-down blue tempera paint and a large paintbrush. Let children know it is okay to paint directly on top of the rainbow, because the crayon wax prevents the paint from soaking in. Set the papers aside to dry.

3 Place different colors of paint on separate paper plates. Explain that you will now use a special **printmaking** technique to make flowers on the ground beneath the rainbow. Demonstrate how to dip the "petals" of the paper towel roll into one color of paint.

4 After thinking aloud about where to place the first flower, press the paper towel roll (paint side down) on the paper to print it. Hold the roll with one hand, and with the other, press down each petal to ensure that it prints.

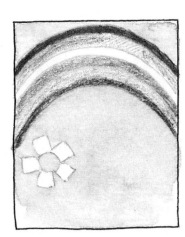

Tip

To avoid muddying the paper towel printers with different colors, set up a table of paint for each color of paint used. Have children move from table to table to print each flower.

5 Explain that you will print a **series** of flowers. Again, think aloud about where the second flower should go, and explain that you want to create an interesting **composition**. Then use another paper towel roll to print the second flower in a different color. Continue in this way until there are three or more flowers of different colors on the page. Encourage children to create their own compositions as they print their flowers.

6 When children have finished printing, encourage them to complete the compositions by painting additional details such as stems, leaves, grass, and clouds.

One Step More

Invite children to think of other materials that might make interesting printmaking tools. Set aside time to try them out.

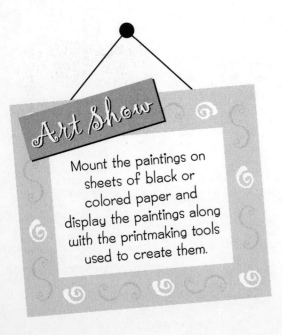

Art Show

Mount the paintings on sheets of black or colored paper and display the paintings along with the printmaking tools used to create them.

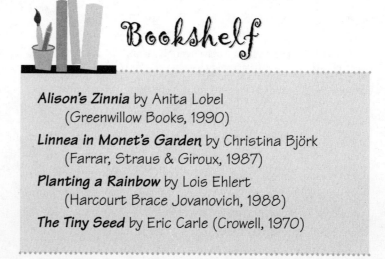

Bookshelf

Alison's Zinnia by Anita Lobel (Greenwillow Books, 1990)

Linnea in Monet's Garden by Christina Björk (Farrar, Straus & Giroux, 1987)

Planting a Rainbow by Lois Ehlert (Harcourt Brace Jovanovich, 1988)

The Tiny Seed by Eric Carle (Crowell, 1970)

Apple Tree Painting and Printing

Children paint and print apple tree pictures.

Materials

- pictures of apple trees during each season
- newspaper
- 11- by 18-inch heavy white paper
- stiff easel paintbrushes
- tempera paint (brown, green, red)
- water containers
- foam trays
- apple-shaped sponges, about 1 1/2 inches wide
- 18- by 24-inch green construction paper
- glue
- 6 apples (optional)
- white tempera paint (optional)

New Art Words

structure

stippling

print

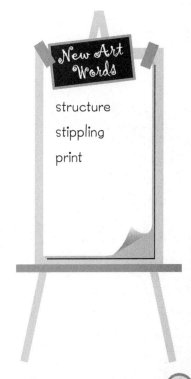

 Let's Begin

Show pictures of apple trees and discuss their **structure**, noting that the branches grow out to the sides rather than straight up. Talk about how farmers prune the trees so the branches grow out. This makes the apples easier to pick. Introduce the technique of **stippling**, which will be used to create the leaves. Stippling is done by bouncing an easel brush up and down on the paper, using only a small amount of paint.

Cover all work surfaces with newspaper. Then pass out the materials and demonstrate the following procedures as children follow along.

Step by Step

1 Demonstrate how to paint a tree trunk with brown paint on white paper. Begin at the base and work upward. Compare the structure of a tree to the skeleton of the human body.

2 Add branches to the trunk, forming a *Y* for the smaller branches. Let the paint dry.

3 Demonstrate the stippling technique, which will be used to paint the leaves. Dab a small amount of green paint on top of the branches to create a leafy texture. Hold the brush straight up and down and bounce the brush. NOTE: Very little paint is needed for stippling.

4 Using an upward motion of the brush, paint grass at the bottom of the paper. Again, very little paint is needed. Allow the paint to dry.

5 Pour red paint into the foam trays. Dip the apple sponges into the red paint to print apples on the tree. **NOTE:** The sponges should be damp but not too wet. Very little paint is needed.

6 Mount the apple tree painting on 18- by 24-inch green construction paper.

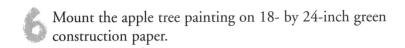
One Step More

Show children how to use real apples to **print** a border. Cut the apples in half crosswise to reveal the star pattern in the middle. Set the cut apples on a paper towel for an hour to absorb the moisture. Place red tempera paint in foam trays and use a piece of apple to print a border around the painting. Make sure there is no excess paint on the apple before printing.

Bookshelf

The Apple Pie Tree by Zoe Hall (Scholastic, 1996)

Cider Apples by Sandy Nightingale (Harcourt Brace & Co., 1996)

The Seasons of Arnold's Apple Tree by Gail Gibbons (Harcourt Brace Jovanovich, 1984)

Art Show

Hang the completed paintings along with several photos of apple trees.

Symmetrical Turtles

Children learn about symmetry as they layer construction paper to create a turtle.

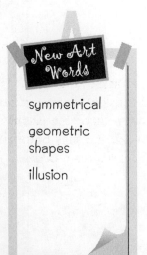

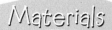

Materials

- 🎨 pictures of various types of turtles
- 🎨 9- by 12-inch construction paper (various colors)
- 🎨 pencils
- 🎨 scissors
- 🎨 glue
- 🎨 12- by 12-inch white drawing paper
- 🎨 4- by 8-inch construction paper (various colors)
- 🎨 markers

New Art Words

symmetrical

geometric shapes

illusion

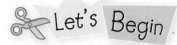 **Let's Begin**

Show children pictures of turtles and point out the designs on their shells. Explain that the designs on the shells form patterns, because they repeat. Then explain that the designs are the same on both sides of the turtle, making the shell **symmetrical**. Help children look for **geometric shapes** such as circles, squares, and rectangles on the turtle shells.

Pass out the materials. Then demonstrate the following procedures as children follow along.

Step by Step

1 Fold a 9- by 12-inch sheet of colored construction paper in half vertically.

2 Place your pencil on the fold, an inch from the top of the paper. Draw a large curved line that ends on the fold, about an inch from the bottom of the paper. The curved line should create half of an oval.

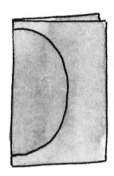

3 Keeping the paper folded, cut along the curved line. Explain that the oval shape will be the turtle's shell.

4 Glue the shell to the center of the white paper.

5 For the feet, choose two small pieces of construction paper that are a different color from the shell. (The two sheets should be the same color.) Fold a sheet in half and draw a *U* shape on one side. Keeping the paper folded, cut out the *U* shape. Repeat with the other sheet of paper. Glue the feet onto the shell, as shown.

⌣ Tip ⌣

To attach the turtle's head, legs, and tail, slip the ends of the pieces under the shell before gluing them down.

6 Select another small sheet of construction paper that is a different color from the shell and feet. Draw a large *U* on the paper to create the turtle's head. Cut out the head and glue onto one end of the shell. Cut out a small triangle from any color paper. Glue it onto the shell for the turtle's tail.

7 Have children cut out geometric shapes to create patterns on their turtle shell. To create a more interesting effect, they might layer smaller shapes on top of the larger ones. Remind children to position their shapes so they form a symmetrical pattern. Glue the shapes into place. Draw two eyes.

8 With a marker, draw an outline around the turtle, as shown. Following this outline, draw another line close to the first line but not touching it. Continue this procedure until you reach the edge of the paper. Explain that these lines will create an **illusion** of water and movement.

One Step More

Invite children to create clay turtles and then paint geometric patterns on the shells.

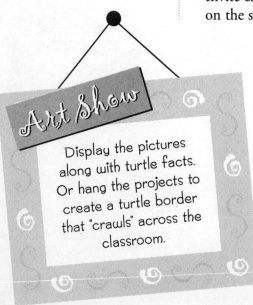

Art Show

Display the pictures along with turtle facts. Or hang the projects to create a turtle border that "crawls" across the classroom.

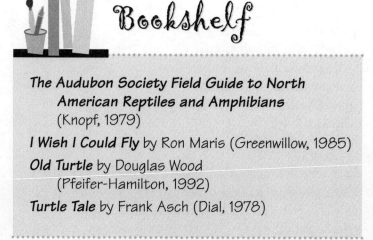

Bookshelf

The Audubon Society Field Guide to North American Reptiles and Amphibians (Knopf, 1979)

I Wish I Could Fly by Ron Maris (Greenwillow, 1985)

Old Turtle by Douglas Wood (Pfeifer-Hamilton, 1992)

Turtle Tale by Frank Asch (Dial, 1978)

Ladybug Rings

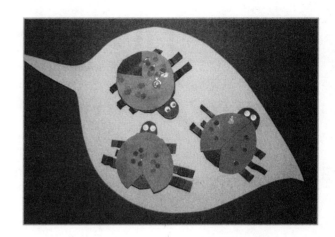

Children create paper ladybug rings that they can wear on their fingers.

Materials

- 🐞 pictures of ladybugs
- 🐞 3- by 1/2-inch black construction paper strips
- 🐞 tape
- 🐞 4- by 4-inch black and red construction paper squares
- 🐞 light-colored crayons or white chalk
- 🐞 scissors
- 🐞 3 1/2- by 1/4-inch black construction paper strips
- 🐞 glue
- 🐞 black crayons
- 🐞 small black construction paper circles (made with a hole punch)
- 🐞 moveable eyes or small white circles

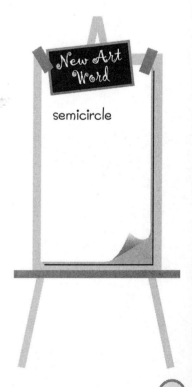

New Art Word

semicircle

Let's Begin

Display pictures of ladybugs and ask children where they might see these creatures. Mention that gardeners like ladybugs because they eat insects that are harmful to plants. Tell children that they will each make a special ring that they can wear—it will look like a ladybug has landed on their hand!

In advance, prepare a paper ring for each child by taping together the ends of a 3- by 1/2-inch black paper strip. Then pass out the materials and demonstrate the following procedures as children follow along.

Step by Step

Tip

Have children use white chalk or a light-colored crayon to trace the circle so that it's visible.

1 Draw or trace a 3-inch circle on a black paper square. (You may wish to make several circle templates in advance for children to share. See page 26 for a circle template.) Cut out the circle.

2 Use three black paper strips for the ladybug's legs. Place them on the black circle so that the legs extend past the circle on each side. Glue the legs into place.

3 Trace the circle template onto a red paper square. Cut out the circle.

4 With a black crayon, draw a letter *Y* so that the ends of the letter touch the edges of the red circle.

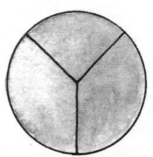

5 Turn the circle so the *Y* is upside down. Cut out the small triangle and discard it.

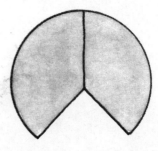

6 Glue the remaining part of the red circle onto the black circle.

7 Glue the small black circles onto the ladybug's back.

8 Cut out a small **semicircle** from black paper. Glue it in place for the ladybug's head.

9 Glue two moveable eyes onto the head. If children are using white paper circles instead, have them draw black pupils.

10 Glue the ladybug onto a black paper ring.

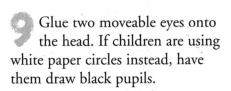

Invite children to make rings representing other insects, birds, or animals.

Bookshelf

The Grouchy Ladybug by Eric Carle (Crowell Co., 1977)

The Icky Bug Alphabet Book by Jerry Pallotta (Charlesbridge, 1986)

The Ladybug and Other Insects by Gallimard Jeunesse and Pascale de Bourgoing (Scholastic, 1991)

Art Show

Have children use their ladybug rings as finger puppets. Encourage children to create dialogue for ladybug skits.

Feathered Friend

Children collaborate to create a large colorful bird. Using found objects and tempera paint, children use printmaking techniques to make the bird's tail feathers.

Materials

- pictures of different types of birds
- 4- by 18-inch white drawing paper
- pencils
- scissors
- tempera paint (various colors)
- paper plates
- objects for printing (such as spools, wood blocks, cardboard pieces, and cut sponges)
- bird body template (page 47)
- 9- by 11-inch colored construction paper, plus scraps
- tape or glue

New Art Words

cool colors

warm colors

printmaking

repetition

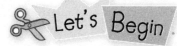 Let's Begin

Display pictures or photographs of different types of birds. Draw children's attention to the various shapes, sizes, and colors of the different tail feathers. Appeal to children's senses by asking questions, such as "How might tail feathers feel if you were able to touch them?" Tell children they will make a large turkey with many beautiful tail feathers. Introduce **warm colors** such as orange, red, yellow, and brown. (You could also create a peacock by changing the body and using **cool colors** such as blue, purple, and green.)

In advance, draw a large feather template in the shape shown on page 45. A suggested size is 18 inches long and 3 or 4 inches wide. Make enough copies of the template for children to share, and cut out the templates.

Pass out the materials. Then demonstrate the following procedures as children follow along.

Step by Step

1 Demonstrate how to trace around the template with pencil on white paper.

2 Pour paints into paper plates. Model how to use the objects for **printmaking**. Dip an object in paint. (Use an extra paper plate to hold the wet printing objects.) Press the object down on the tail feather. Encourage children to repeat the design they are using in different areas within the tail feather. Explain that this is called **repetition**. (If using sponges, cut them into shapes. Then wet them and wring out the extra water before printing. Only a small amount of paint is needed.)

3 After the first color has dried, choose a second shape and use a different color to print additional patterns. Point out that the use of the same shapes dipped in different colors also creates an interesting design.

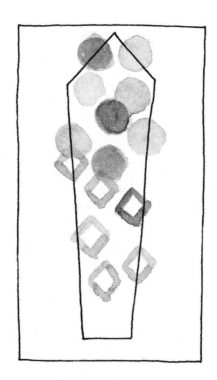

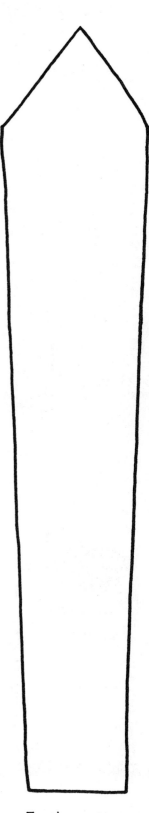

Feather pattern

4 Encourage children to fill their tail feathers with many different shapes and colors.

5 When the paint has dried, have children cut out the feathers along the pencil lines.

One Step More

Using the template on page 47, cut out a bird body from any color paper. Add a construction paper beak, eyes, and feet. If desired, draw rows of feathers across the body. Assemble the tail feathers in a fan shape around the body, overlapping the tail feathers slightly. Attach the feathers to the back of the body with tape or glue. Display the bird as the centerpiece of a colorful bulletin board titled "Meet Our Feathered Friend."

Art Show

Have children write or dictate statements about the bird or the printmaking process, and add them to your Feathered Friend bulletin board display.

Bookshelf

Hey, Al by Arthur Yorinks
(Farrar, Straus & Giroux, 1986)

Rainbow Crow: A Lenape Tale by Nancy Van Laan
(Knopf, 1989)

Raven by Gerald McDermott
(Harcourt Brace, 1993)

Tico and the Golden Wings by Leo Lionni
(Pantheon, 1964)

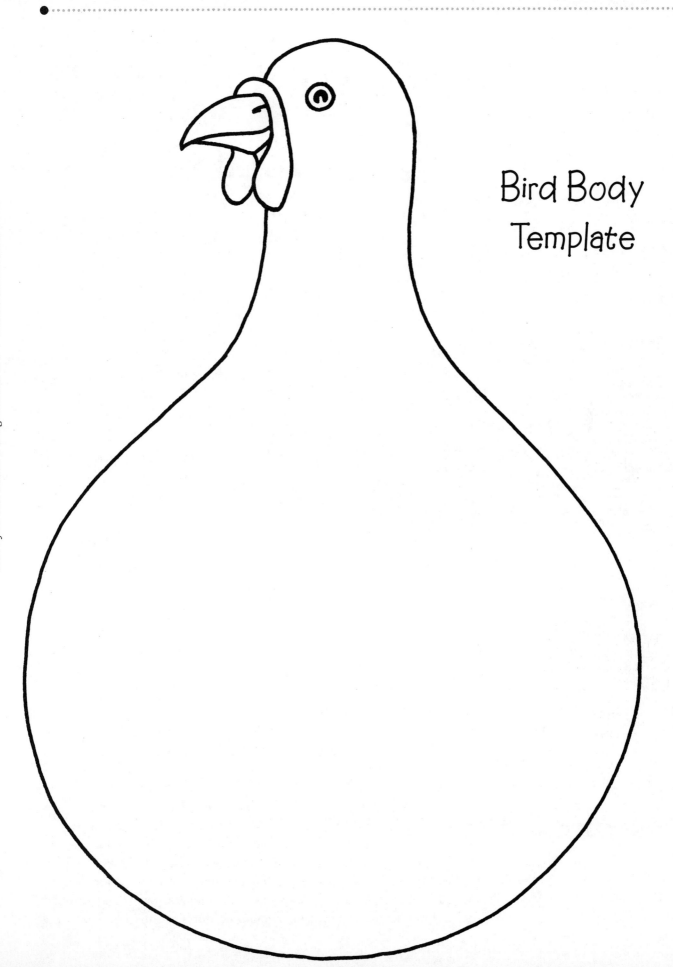

Bird Body
Template

Colorful Collage Creatures

Children create a collage of imaginative animals using finger-painted papers.

Materials
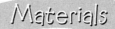

- pictures of various animals
- patterns of geometric shapes
- newspaper
- finger-paint paper
- finger paint (red, yellow, and blue)
- old combs, forks, and cardboard scraps
- pencils and dark crayons
- scissors
- glue
- 12- by 18-inch white construction paper

New Art Words

geometric shapes

collage

primary colors

secondary colors

texture

finger paint

outline

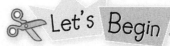

Let's Begin

Show children illustrations and photographs of domestic and wild animals. Discuss the range of colors of these animals. Ask children about the different habitats or surroundings of the animals in the pictures. Encourage children to think about simple **geometric shapes** that they might use to create pictures of these animals. For example, you might say, "Imagine a circle for a head and an oval for a body. Could you use a triangle for a leg? How about squares and rectangles?" Tell children that they will make **collages** by using painted geometric shapes to form colorful creatures.

In advance, prepare templates of geometric shapes such as ovals, rectangles, circles, and triangles. Make these shapes large and simple. Make small and medium shapes as well so that children can use these for their animal's head or legs. Cover work surfaces with newspaper. Then pass out materials and demonstrate the following procedures as children follow along.

(Activity continued on page 49.)

Watercolor Buildings

Shaping Houses ▶

Torn-Paper Landscapes

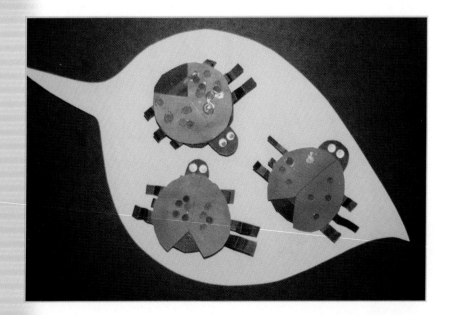

Step by Step

1 Demonstrate how to mix **primary colors** (red, blue, and yellow) to create **secondary colors**. (Red and blue = purple; red and yellow = orange; blue and yellow = green; red, blue, and yellow = brown)

2 Have children write their names on the back of their finger-paint paper. Explain that children will first create the **texture** of their animal. Spoon primary colors of **finger paint** onto each child's paper. Model how to use the paint to create expressive textures on

the paper. For example, demonstrate how to use your fingers in the paint to create straight lines, curved lines, wiggles, scribbles, patterns, and shapes. Show how to use a comb, fork, or scraps of cardboard to make interesting textures. Let the finger paintings dry on newspaper overnight.

3 On the back of the dry painted papers, show children how to trace the shape templates to form the shape of an animal. Have children decide on an animal and arrange the templates to create its shape.

BACK OF PAINTED PAPER

∽ **Tip** ∽

Have children rinse their hands in soapy washtubs before they use the sink. Make cleanup a lesson in following directions, saying "Hold your hands in the air. Do not touch anything on your way to the rinse bucket!"

TRACE OUTLINE, THEN CUT OUT

4 Trace over or around the entire animal **outline** using a dark crayon. This makes it easier to see the CUT line. Cut out the animal in one piece. NOTE: Save the scraps for step 6.

5 Glue the animal onto white construction paper. Then tell children to think about an environment or background for their animal. Ask: "Where would your animal feel comfortable? Do you know what type of habitat your animal needs to survive?"

6 Have children share their scraps from their finger paintings. Invite them to cut out shapes to represent water, grass, trees, rocks, clouds, and sky. Children can glue these pieces onto the background to create a multicolored setting for their animal.

One Step More

Show children examples of illustrators and artists, such as Eric Carle, who use collage techniques in their work.

Art Show

Have children write poems or stories about their creatures. Display these along with their finished artwork.

Bookshelf

Beast Feast by Doug Florian
(Harcourt Brace, 1994)

Draw 50 Endangered Animals by Lee J. Ames
(Doubleday, 1992)

Eric Carle's Animals, Animals by Eric Carle
(Philomel Books, 1989)

Today Is Monday by Eric Carle
(Philomel Books, 1993)

In the Doghouse

**Every child will have a pet dog—
in its own doghouse—when this project
is completed!**

Materials

- pictures of dogs and/or stuffed toy dogs
- dog template (page 54, optional)
- 9- by 12-inch heavy white paper
- pencils
- black crayons and markers
- watercolor paints
- paintbrushes
- water containers
- scissors
- 4- by 12-inch strips of colored construction paper
- 12- by 18-inch white drawing paper
- glue
- colored markers or crayons

New Art Words

outline

watercolor wash

value

palette

arch

 Let's Begin

Read aloud a story about a dog (see suggestions under Bookshelf). Show pictures of dogs and/or stuffed toy dogs. Ask children to describe the kinds of dogs they have as pets or have seen. Talk about the different colors of dogs.

In advance, cut out enough dog templates for children to share (optional). Pass out the materials and demonstrate the following procedures as children follow along.

Step by Step

1 Trace the template in the center of a sheet of 9- by 12-inch paper. The large part of the template should be at the bottom of the page. Explain that this shape will be the body of a dog. Or have children draw a large dog on their own.

2 Using the pictures or stuffed animals for reference, guide children through the look-and-draw technique to complete a drawing of a dog. Add ears, a nose and mouth, eyes, paws, and a tail. Include a few spots and other details.

3 Use a black crayon to **outline** the pencil drawing.

4 Demonstrate how to use watercolor paints with a wet brush and a little paint to create a **watercolor wash**. Show children how to make a darker **value** by adding more paint to the wet brush. Display the **palette** of watercolors, and suggest that children create a fanciful painting using brown, yellow, blue, or any color of their choice. Have children paint their dogs. Allow the paintings to dry, and then cut out the dogs.

5 Choose two paper strips to make a three-dimensional roof for the doghouse. Glue the short ends together to form a long strip, and let the glue dry. Cut a one-inch slit in the center of the strip. Then fold the

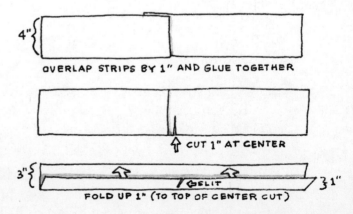

4" OVERLAP STRIPS BY 1" AND GLUE TOGETHER

⬆ CUT 1" AT CENTER

3" SLIT ⅓ 1"
FOLD UP 1" (TO TOP OF CENTER CUT)

bottom inch of the strip back all the way along the strip. (Show students how the top of the slit shows them where to fold.) Children will need extra guidance for steps 5 and 6.

6 Bend the strip at the slit to form the roof. Put glue along the one-inch fold and glue to the top of a sheet of 12- by 18-inch paper. Discuss the three-dimensional peak and roof overhang that results.

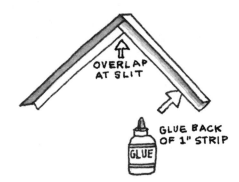

7 Cut off the corners of the large paper behind the roof.

8 Use a marker to draw a large **arch** for a door opening. Add horizontal lines for clapboards. Glue the dog to the center of the door.

One Step More

Encourage children to use markers or crayons to add grass, a dog dish, a bone, or other details to their doghouses.

Bookshelf

Biscuit Finds a Friend by Alyssa Satin Capucilli (HarperCollins, 1997)

Clifford, We Love You by Norman Bridwell (Scholastic, 1991) and other books in the Clifford series

If Dogs Had Wings by Larry Dane Brimner (Boyds Mills Press, 1996)

Pinkerton, Behave! by Steven Kellogg (Dial Press, 1979)

Sheepdog in the Snow by Lucy Daniels (Barron's Educational Series, 1996)

Art Show

Exhibit children's dogs in a hall display case. Include stuffed toy dogs to enhance the display.

Dog Template

Art Projects That Dazzle & Delight: Grades K–1 Scholastic Professional Books

Self-Portraits

**Children express their unique artistic styles
and personalities as they create self-portraits.**

Materials

- examples of self-portraits
- 10-inch oval templates
- 9- by 12-inch construction paper (colors of various skin tones)
- pencils
- scissors
- 12- by 18-inch white or colored construction paper
- glue
- mirrors, if available
- fine-tipped markers
- yarn (brown, black, tan, yellow, and orange)

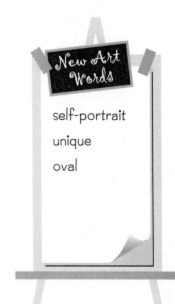

New Art Words

self-portrait

unique

oval

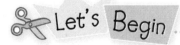 Let's Begin

Show examples of **self-portraits** by artists such as Vincent Van Gogh, Rembrandt, Pablo Picasso, and Albrecht Dürer. Explain that many artists paint portraits of themselves. Help children identify some of the details and techniques that make each self-portrait as unique as the person who created it. Talk about some of the things that make people **unique**, or "one of a kind."

In advance, create enough 10-inch **oval** templates for children to share. Pass out materials and demonstrate the following procedures as children follow along.

Step by Step

1 Discuss the oval shape of a face, noting that an oval is rounded on top and bottom but more narrow on the sides than a circle. Have children choose a sheet of colored paper for their self-portrait. Trace the oval template onto the paper and cut it out. Demonstrate how to cut out a neck and ears from the extra paper.

2 Glue the oval head, neck, and ears onto a large sheet of white or colored paper.

3 Talk about where facial features are located in relation to one another. Have children close their eyes and lightly touch their face, feeling how their eyes are halfway between the top of their head and chin and how the top of the nose fits in between the eyes. Have them feel the distance between the nose and mouth and between the mouth and chin. Provide mirrors, if available, and encourage children to observe their facial features.

4 Have children imagine drawing a line halfway between the top of the head and the chin. Explain that the eyes go here—not at the top of the oval. Use marker or pencil to draw one eye in the shape of a football. Show children how to use two fingers to measure the space between the eyes, and then draw the second eye. Add a color for the iris and a black pupil. Draw eyelashes on the top and bottom of the eyes. (If drawing in pencil, outline in black marker when finished.)

5 Demonstrate how to draw several different nose shapes. Have children draw a nose, starting between the eyes.

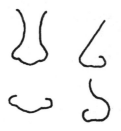

6 Leave a space the width of a finger between the nose and the upper lip. Draw a wavy line for the top lip and a curved line, like a smile, for the bottom lip. Draw a straight line for the middle of the lips.

7 Have children select a color of yarn that is close to their own hair color. Show them how to cut pieces and glue them in place.

8 Draw a line extending from the neck to the edge of the paper to form shoulders. Then draw a collar, and color the shirt or decorate it with a pattern. Encourage children to draw their favorite shirt.

One Step More

Use the portraits as a way to introduce children to one another at the beginning of the school year. Add speech balloons to have each portrait "tell" the class something about the artist.

Bookshelf

Li'l Sis and Uncle Willie: A Story Based on the Life and Painting of William H. Johnson by Gwen Everett (Rizzoli International, 1991)

Looking at Paintings: Children by Peggy Roalf (Hyperion Books for Children, 1993)

Mary Cassatt by Mike Venezia (Children's Press, 1990)

People by Peter Spier (Doubleday, 1980)

Picasso by Mike Venezia (Children's Press, 1988)

Art Show

For parents' night, tape a ruler to the back of each portrait. Tape the portraits to chairs so that your "students" can greet visitors!

Funny Face Masks

Children create a three-dimensional paper mask using folding, cutting, and pasting techniques.

Materials

- masks or pictures of masks from different cultures
- 9- by 12-inch construction paper (various colors)
- pencils
- scissors
- 4- by 6-inch pieces of construction paper (various colors)
- glue and tape
- crayons or markers
- black markers
- 1- by 3-inch black construction paper rectangles
- 3- by 3-inch construction paper squares (various colors)
- 2- by 3-inch red or pink construction paper rectangles
- 1- by 12-inch strips of construction paper (various colors)

New Art Words

accordion fold

three-dimensional

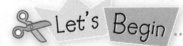 Let's Begin ⋯⋯⋯⋯⋯⋯⋯⋯⋯⋯⋯⋯⋯⋯⋯⋯⋯⋯⋯⋯⋯⋯⋯⋯

Show students pictures or examples of masks from different cultures. Discuss why people make masks and when they wear them. Point out that many African and Native American masks are worn for important ceremonies. Some masks are worn to tell a story, and some are worn just for fun on occasions, such as Halloween and Mardi Gras.

   In advance, create enough 10-inch oval templates for children to share. Then pass out materials and demonstrate the following procedures as children follow along.

Step by Step

1 Place the oval template on a sheet of construction paper. With a pencil, trace the oval and then cut it out.

2 Choose a 4- by 6-inch rectangle and fold it in half lengthwise. Draw a dot on each side, as shown. To create an eye shape, draw two curved lines that connect the two dots. Keeping the paper folded, carefully cut out the eyes.

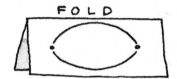

3 Glue the eyes to the middle of the face. Select a crayon or marker to color the eyes. For the iris, draw a circle in the middle of each eye. With black marker, draw a small circle in the middle of each iris for the pupil.

4 Use two black paper rectangles for the eyelashes. Snip along the longer edge of the rectangles, stopping about a quarter-inch from the top of the rectangle. Make each cut close to the one before it. Curl the eyelashes around a pencil or gently fold them up. Glue them above the eyes. (Or, draw the eyelashes with black marker.)

5 For the nose, select a paper square of any color. Demonstrate different nose shapes: triangle, oval, or a more realistic shape with nostrils. Cut out the nose and glue it in place.

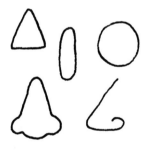

6 Draw lips on a red or pink rectangle. Begin with a dot on each side, as you did for the eyes. Draw a curved line to connect the dots for the lower lip. Draw a line with two bumps for the upper lip. Cut out the lips and glue them onto the face.

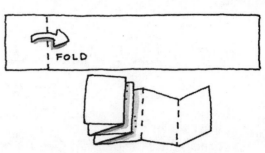

7 Demonstrate an **accordion fold**. Take a strip of paper and begin by folding an inch of the far end toward you. Holding this folded piece, make another fold of the same size, this time folding away from you. As you continue to fold, have children take strips and try it. Explain that you are making hair. Glue the hair around the face. Hold the hair in place for ten seconds to help it stay in place.

8 Next, give the mask a **three-dimensional** shape. At the bottom of the mask, cut two slits that look like a small triangle. Pull the two sides together and tape them. Repeat at the top of the mask.

One Step More

Following the same procedures, create masks of animals or imaginary creatures.

Art Show

Children can wear their masks by cutting holes to see through and adding string to fit around their heads. Have children model their masks!

Bookshelf

Can You See the Leopard? African Masks by Christine Stelzig and Fiona Elliot (Neeves Publishing, 1997)

Costume Crafts by Iain MacLeod-Brudenell (Gareth Stevens, 1994)

Cut and Make African Masks in Full Color by Albert Gary Smith and Josie Hazen (Dover, 1993 and 1991)

Indian Masks: Punch-Out Designs by Albert Gary Smith and Josie Hazen (Dover, 1991)

Masks of Mexico: Tigers, Devils, and the Dance of Life by Barbara Maudlin (Museum of New Mexico Press, 1999)

Fictitious Faces

This project combines math and art lessons as children create abstract portraits using geometric shapes.

Materials

- examples of paintings by Paul Klee
- 9- by 12-inch heavy white paper
- black crayons
- paintbrushes
- water containers
- tissue paper (the type that bleeds, various colors)
- 10- by 14-inch black or colored construction paper (optional, for mounting)

New Art Words

geometric shapes

vertical

horizontal

realistic

abstract

overlapping

 Let's Begin

Explain that the inspiration for this project comes from the artist Paul Klee. Show children examples of his work as well as abstract portraits by other artists. Talk about the way **geometric shapes** can be used to form a face.

Pass out the materials. Then demonstrate the following procedures as children follow along.

Step by Step

1 Place a sheet of white paper in a **vertical** position. Using black crayon, draw a large circle for a head. Starting at the jaw, draw lines for the neck and shoulders.

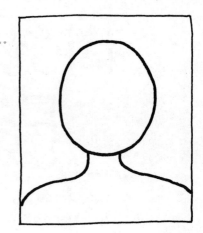

2 Show examples of different geometric shapes, and discuss how they might be used for the details or designs on the face, neck, and shoulders.

3 Draw a **horizontal** line through the middle of the large circle. Add a second line below it, as shown.

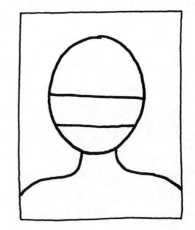

4 Draw a line that divides the head in half vertically.

5 Draw ovals for the eyes on the top horizontal line. Make half the oval above the line and half below.

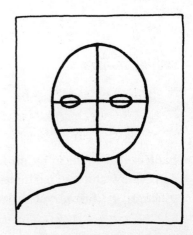

6 Have children draw geometric shapes of their choice for the nose and mouth.

7 Add other geometric shapes to the neck and shoulders to create interesting details or designs. Explain that this helps to break up large areas of space. Children may also add ears. Point out that the finished drawings do not look **realistic**; they have an **abstract** quality.

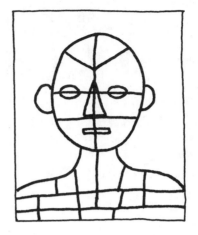

8 Using a paintbrush, wet the surface of the paper. Place torn pieces of colored tissue paper on top of the wet area, and use the brush to wet the top of the tissue paper. Explain that when water is added, the color from the tissue paper will bleed through onto the paper beneath it. Encourage the **overlapping** of tissue paper to create interesting new colors. Once dry, the tissue paper will fall off and beautiful colors will be left.

WATER

TORN COLORED TISSUE PAPER

One Step More

Read aloud *Paul Klee* by Mike Venezia (Children's Press, 1991) or other books about Paul Klee. Discuss his painting techniques, such as his use of colors and shapes.

Bookshelf

Colors: A First Discovery Book by Gallimard Jeunesse and Pascale de Bourgoing (Scholastic, 1991)

The Incredible Painting of Felix Clousseau by Jon Agee (Farrar, Straus & Giroux, 1988)

Shapes, Shapes, Shapes by Tana Hoban (Greenwillow Books, 1986)

When Pigasso Met Mootisse by Nina Laden (Chronicle Books, 1998)

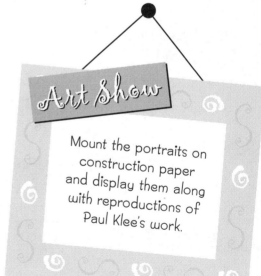

Art Show

Mount the portraits on construction paper and display them along with reproductions of Paul Klee's work.

Wild Things

Children create imaginative monsters using tempera paint and folded paper.

Materials

- newspaper
- 12- by 18-inch tagboard or heavy white paper
- pencils
- tempera paint (red, blue, and yellow)
- paintbrushes (various sizes)
- water containers
- medium and small easel paintbrushes
- scissors
- 1- by 12-inch construction paper strips (red, blue, and yellow)
- glue
- tape

New Art Words

primary colors

accordion folding

curling

three-dimensional

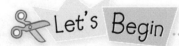
Let's Begin

Discuss the features of a monster face, such as enlarged eyes, nose, and mouth; pointed teeth; stringy hair; or colored fur. Have children recall monsters from picture books. Discuss how some artists combine characteristics of different animals to create monsters—for example, the feet of a chicken, the horns of a goat, and the face of a lion. Explain that children will paint their own monster face using **primary colors** (red, blue, and yellow).

In advance, cover several tables with newspaper. Set up paint stations, one color on each table. Then pass out the materials and demonstrate the following procedures as children follow along.

Step by Step

1 Draw a large head, using pencil on tagboard. Make the head large enough to fill the tagboard. Add eyes, nose, and a mouth, as well as teeth, ears, and horns. Encourage children to use their imagination.

2 Paint the head and facial features. Assign children to a paint station. Have them stay at that station until you give a signal. Then have students move to the next station. Allow several minutes at each station. Explain that the brushes must be left at each paint station to prevent the mixing of colors. Encourage children to use smaller brushes to paint details.

3 Allow the paintings to dry. Have children cut out the monster faces.

4 Using the colored paper strips, demonstrate **accordion folding** and paper **curling** techniques. (See page 60 for accordion-folding directions. To curl paper, tightly wind a strip around a pencil.) Glue the strips onto the face for hair, beards, or fur.

WRAP PAPER AROUND PENCIL

One Step More

Give the wild thing a **three-dimensional** effect by cutting a slit in the bottom of the face. Overlap the edges and tape them together.

⇧ CUT SLIT, OVERLAP, AND TAPE

Bookshelf

Mercer Mayer's A Monster Followed Me to School by Mercer Mayer (Golden Book, 1991)

The Monster Under My Bed by Suzanne Gruber (Troll, 1997)

One Monster After Another by Mercer Mayer (Golden Press, 1974)

Where the Wild Things Are by Maurice Sendak (Harper & Row, 1963)

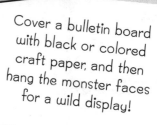

Art Show

Cover a bulletin board with black or colored craft paper, and then hang the monster faces for a wild display!

Ice Cream Colors

Children capture the flavors of summer by creating giant paper ice cream cones.

Materials

- 12- by 18-inch brown paper (craft paper, construction paper, or paper bags)
- markers or crayons
- scissors
- 9- by 12-inch construction paper (various unusual colors, such as turquoise, magenta, or mint green)
- glue
- small scraps of red paper

New Art Words

cyan

turquoise

magenta

vertical

horizontal

texture

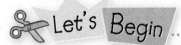 Let's Begin

Ask children to close their eyes and imagine an ice cream cone. Ask: "What colors do you see? How does ice cream feel? How does it taste?" Show children colors whose names they may not know, such as **cyan** and **turquoise**. Ask kids what ice cream flavors might come in these colors. For example, cyan could be blueberry ice cream and **magenta** could be raspberry or cherry. Tell children that they will make giant ice cream cones of any flavor they can imagine.

Pass out the materials. Then demonstrate the following procedures as children follow along.

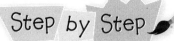
Step by Step

1 Demonstrate an easy way to draw a cone. Make crayon marks in the top two corners of the brown paper and a third mark in the middle of the bottom edge of the paper. Connect the marks with two lines to form a triangle.

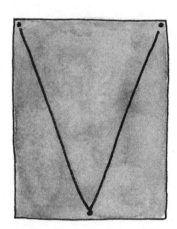

2 Using crayon or marker, draw about six **vertical** lines inside the cone. Describe these lines as "standing tall." Draw about six **horizontal** lines crossing over the first lines so that the pattern of the lines resembles the **texture** of an ice cream cone. Cut out the cone.

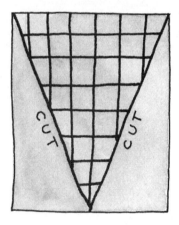

3 Invite children to choose at least three colors they would like to use to represent ice cream flavors. Tell children the names of the colors.

4 Demonstrate how to draw cloud-shaped ice cream scoops. Have children draw and then cut out three different scoops.

5 Put a thin line of glue along the top edge of the ice cream cone, and attach the first scoop. Then put a thin line of glue along the top of the first scoop. Attach the second scoop. Follow the same procedure to attach the third scoop to the second one.

6 Top the cone with a small red paper circle for a cherry. Use markers or crayons to draw sprinkles.

One Step More

Children might add details to their cones, using materials such as glitter, scraps of paper, or birdseed for chunky ice cream.

Art Show

Have children write poems in the shape of ice cream cones. Display the poems along with their artwork on a hallway bulletin board.

Bookshelf

Colors: A First Discovery Book by Gallimard Jeunesse and Pascale de Bourgoing (Scholastic, 1991)

"I Did Not Eat Your Ice Cream" from *Something Big Has Been Here* by Jack Prelutsky (Greenwillow Books, 1990)

Sun Dancers

**Celebrate the coming of summer
with a sun mobile made from crepe paper
streamers and crayons.**

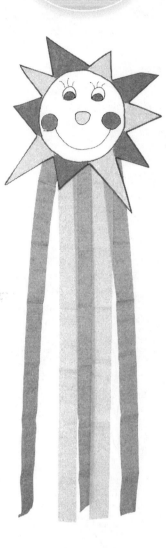

Materials

- 12- by 12-inch white tagboard or heavy white drawing paper
- pencils
- markers
- crayons (fluorescent or bright colors)
- scissors
- crepe paper streamers or large sheets of tissue paper cut into long strips (red, yellow, and orange)
- glue
- string or yarn (optional)

New Art Words

mobile
exaggerated
fluorescent
warm colors

Let's Begin

Ask children to describe how the sun makes them feel. List some of their ideas on the chalkboard. Ask children if they know what a **mobile** is (a hanging sculpture that usually has parts that move in the wind). Then tell children that they will make a large sun mobile with colorful rays that will move when they hold it outdoors.

Pass out the materials and demonstrate the following procedures as children follow along.

Step by Step

1 Use a pencil to draw a large circle on the tagboard, leaving room on all sides for the sun's rays. Then draw pointed or rounded rays all around the circle. Tell children that if they would like, they can make the rays different heights and widths. In the center, draw a cartoon face with **exaggerated** facial features. Outline the drawing in marker.

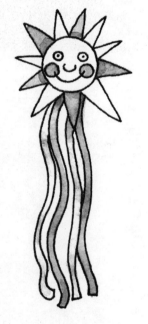

2 Color the rays with **fluorescent** crayons. Introduce or review the concept of **warm colors** (red, orange, and yellow). Discuss things that make you feel warm, such as sunshine and fire. Explain to children that these colors are used in a picture to give the viewer a warm feeling. Children can color the face as well, or they can leave the face white and color the facial features.

3 Cut out the sun. (For safety, trim the pointed rays so that they are not sharp.) Glue several crepe paper streamers to the bottom edge of the sun and let the glue dry.

One Step More

Invite students to use their sun dancers as they dance and sing songs about the sun. This is a fun outdoor activity because the breeze will move the "rays."

Art Show

To display a sun dancer as a mobile, punch a hole at the top and insert string or yarn. Tie a knot to form a loop for hanging.

Bookshelf

Sun Song by Jean Marzollo (HarperCollins, 1995)

Sun Up, Sun Down by Gail Gibbons (Harcourt Brace Jovanovich, 1983)

Welcome Back, Sun by Michael Emberley (Little Brown, 1993)

When the Sun Rose by Barbara Helen Berger (Philomel Books, 1986)

Fall Leaves

**Children mix paint colors
to create a vibrant
autumn tree.**

Materials

- photographs of trees in autumn
- 10- by 16-inch paper (tan, yellow, or orange)
- tempera paints (brown, yellow, red, orange)
- stiff easel brushes (or large paintbrushes)
- water containers
- 12- by 18-inch black or dark-colored paper
  (optional, for mounting)

New Art Words

vertical

stippling

Impressionists

 Let's Begin

Display photographs of fall foliage. Ask: "What happens to the leaves on
the trees during the fall? What happens to leaves during spring? What
about during summer or winter?" Discuss what causes leaves to change
color and fall as the weather gets cooler. Then explain that children will
make a beautiful fall tree to celebrate this colorful season. (You might try
this activity with fluorescent paints in yellow, orange, and pink.)

Pass out the materials. Then demonstrate the following procedures as
children follow along.

Step by Step

1. Place the paper in a **vertical** position. To make a tree trunk, start at the bottom of the page and paint a thick brown line that continues about halfway up the page. Demonstrate how to make branches by adding two more lines (forming a *Y*). To add more branches, make several small *Y*'s extending from the first two branches. Let the paint dry.

2. Explain that you will make leaves by **stippling** the paint with a brush. To stipple, put a small amount of paint on the brush and hold it perpendicular to the paper. Gently bounce the brush on the tree branches, creating dots of color. Move the brush around the tree and on the ground to create the sense of falling leaves.

3. Clean the brush in water, and begin stippling in the same way with the next color of paint. Don't be afraid to let the paint overlap. Ask: "What happens when the yellow and the red paint touch and overlap? Do you see the new color?" Continue in this way until children have finished their trees. Let the paintings dry.

One Step More

Introduce children to the art of the **Impressionists**, a group of nineteenth-century painters who painted colorful "impressions" of the world around them. Display works by Claude Monet, Camille Pissarro, or Auguste Renoir. Invite children to look for stippling paint strokes.

Art Show

Mount children's paintings on black or dark-colored paper. Display the paintings with reproductions of paintings by Impressionists and a few real autumn leaves.

Bookshelf

Autumn Leaves by Ken Robbins (Scholastic Press, 1998)

The Fall of Freddie the Leaf: A Story of Life for All Ages by Leo Buscaglia (Holt, Rinehart and Winston, 1982)

The First Red Maple Leaf by Ludmila Zeman (Tundra Books, 1997)

Red Leaf, Yellow Leaf by Lois Ehlert (Harcourt Brace Jovanovich, 1991)

Why Do Leaves Change Color? by Betsy Maestro (HarperCollins, 1994)

Penguins on Parade

Children create penguins and attach them to a snowy chalk background.

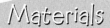
Materials

- pictures of penguins
- 3- by 16-inch tagboard strips
- pencils
- scissors
- 10- by 16-inch dark blue construction paper
- white chalk
- paper towels or tissues
- 3- by 4-inch white drawing paper
- black and orange crayons
- glue
- polyfill or cotton
- 12- by 18-inch white paper (optional, for mounting)

New Art Words

template
horizontal
feathering
profile
foreground
three-dimensional
cool colors

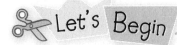
Let's Begin

This activity fits perfectly with a classroom study of Antarctica. Discuss the ice, snow, and glaciers that are part of the penguins' environment. Display pictures of different kinds of penguins for children to observe. Ask children whether they've ever seen penguins in a zoo.

Pass out the materials and demonstrate the following procedures as children follow along.

Step by Step

1 Take a strip of tagboard and draw a curvy line close to the top edge. Cut along this line to form a **template**. Explain that you will use the template to create a snowy landscape for penguins.

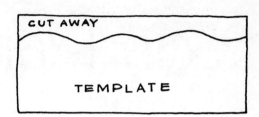

Tip

Place the template at a slight angle to make it look like there are glaciers in the background.

2 Place the blue paper in a **horizontal** position. Rub white chalk along the top inch or so of the curvy edge of the template. Place the template, with the chalk on top, about two inches from the top of the blue paper. Using a paper towel or tissue, rub the chalk in an upward motion only, pushing the chalk in a **feathering**, or soft manner, onto the blue paper. Rub more chalk along the curvy edge of the template and continue to feather it onto the blue paper, moving the template down about two inches each time. Continue chalking to the bottom of the paper. Discard templates and tissues (and have students wash their hands).

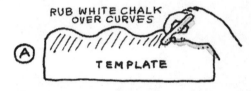

3 Using pencil on 3- by 4-inch white paper, guide children through the look-and-draw process to create several penguins. Draw the **profile**, or side view, of the penguins. Using crayons, color the black parts of the body. Color the beaks and feet orange. Leave the penguins' tummies white. Cut out the penguins.

4 To create snow in the **foreground**, spread white glue across the bottom of the chalked paper, approximately one inch from the bottom. Take a small handful of polyfill or cotton and stretch it to cover the glued area. Press it onto the glued surface to secure. This gives a **three-dimensional** look to the artwork.

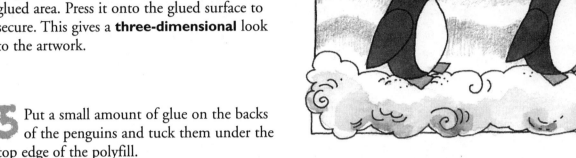

5 Put a small amount of glue on the backs of the penguins and tuck them under the top edge of the polyfill.

One Step More

Students may wish to add penguins in other positions. Some may choose to have the penguins sliding or diving off the icebergs. A northern lights effect can be made using chalk in **cool colors** (blue, green, and violet) on white paper.

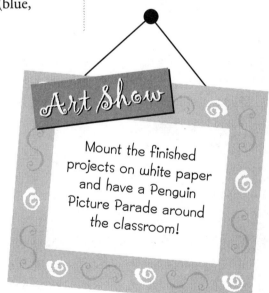

Art Show

Mount the finished projects on white paper and have a Penguin Picture Parade around the classroom!

Bookshelf

Antarctic Antics: A Book of Penguin Poems by Judy Sierra (Harcourt Brace & Co., 1998)

The Penguin by Paula Z. Hogan (Raintree, 1979)

Waiting to Fly: My Escapades With the Penguins of Antarctica by Ron Naveen (Morrow, 1999)

Let It Snow!

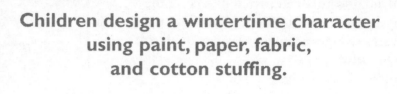

Children design a wintertime character using paint, paper, fabric, and cotton stuffing.

Materials

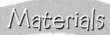

- pictures or photographs of snowflakes
- 12- by 18-inch blue construction paper
- white and black tempera paint
- paintbrushes (various sizes)
- water containers
- fabric scraps
- scissors
- glue
- small orange paper triangles
- polyfill or cotton

New Art Words

unique

overlap

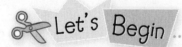 Let's Begin

Read a story about a snowman (see suggestions under Bookshelf), and discuss children's experiences in winter. Ask: "How many of you have ever made a snowman? What happens when the sun comes out?" Display photos or illustrations of snowflakes and discuss how each snowflake is **unique**, or different from any other. Tell children they are going to make a snowman (or woman) that won't melt on the hottest day!

Pass out the materials. Then demonstrate the following procedures as children follow along.

Step by Step

1 Children may choose to position the blue paper horizontally or vertically. (Position it vertically for a tall snowman.) With the white paint, make a bumpy line that looks like fresh, soft snow along the bottom of the paper. Then paint the space below the line white.

2 Explain that you will paint a snowman in a way that is similar to building a real one. The biggest snowball goes on the bottom. Paint a white circle on the snowy ground and fill it in with paint. For the middle, paint a circle sitting on top of the first one. The second circle should be a little smaller and should **overlap** the bottom circle. For the head, add an even smaller circle on top.

3 Paint black dots for eyes, buttons, and a mouth.

4 Cut out the shapes of a hat and scarf from fabric scraps. Glue them onto the snowman. Add an orange triangle for a carrot nose.

~ Tip ~

You may wish to cut fabric hats and scarves in advance.

5 Take a small piece of polyfill or cotton and stretch it until it is long enough to cover the bottom of the page. Spread a thin layer of glue over the snowy ground and gently pat the polyfill in place.

6 Paint white snowflakes in the background. Encourage children to make each snowflake unique, just as real ones are unique.

One Step More

Have children paint a step-by-step sequence showing how to make a snowman.

Art Show

Invite children to write imaginative stories about what happens when their snowmen come to life. Display the stories with children's artwork.

Bookshelf

The Biggest Best Snowman by Margery Cuyler (Scholastic, 1998)

Snow Day by Moira Fain (Walker and Co., 1996)

The Snowman Who Went for a Walk by Mira Lobe (William Morrow, 1984)

Snow on Snow on Snow by Cheryl Chapman (Dial Books for Young Readers, 1994)

The Snowy Day by Ezra Jack Keats (Viking Press, 1962)

Pussy Willow Paintings

This project combines science and art skills as children observe and replicate the patterns of a pussy willow branch.

Materials

- pussy willow branches or pictures of pussy willows
- 10- by 16-inch light blue paper
- pencils
- paintbrushes (various sizes)
- tempera paint (brown, yellow, green, white)
- water containers
- 12- by 18-inch white paper (optional, for mounting)

Let's Begin

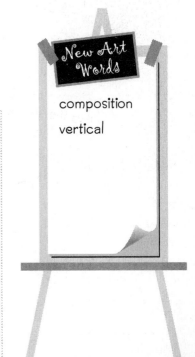

New Art Words

composition

vertical

Display real pussy willow stems (available at florist shops) or pictures of pussy willows. Ask children to observe the graceful patterns of the blossoms, which alternate on each stem. Talk about the stages of plant growth. Ask: "What color do you think first appeared on each bud?" (yellow or green) Draw attention to the soft look of each bud. Ask: "How do you think it would feel?" (very soft, like a furry kitten) Discuss how a group of stems can create a **composition**, or arrangement.

Pass out the materials. Then demonstrate the following procedures as children follow along.

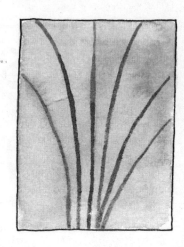

Step by Step

1 Place a sheet of blue paper in a **vertical** position. Using pencil, draw a simple composition of curved lines. Start at the bottom and draw a gently curving line to the top of the paper. Draw five or six branch lines, until the arrangement fills the paper with a graceful flow. Vary the length and direction of lines.

2 Select a small brush to paint brown tempera paint on top of each branch line. Use smooth, continuous brush strokes to cover the lines in a sweeping motion.

3 Select another small brush to paint the base of each pussy willow bud yellow or green. Let the paint dry.

4 Select a large brush (round-tipped, if available) to dab white paint for each pussy willow. Place the white pussy willow dabs next to each bud of yellow or green. Keep the brush full of fresh white paint, and try to avoid smearing or mixing with other colors.

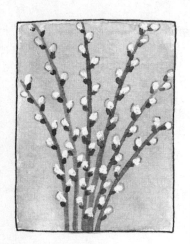

One Step More

Select other natural subjects for observational paintings and drawings.

Art Show

Mount the paintings on white paper. Display them along with real pussy willow branches to illustrate the patterns and colors of spring.

Bookshelf

A Busy Year by Leo Lionni (Knopf, 1992)

The True Book of Buds by Dr. Helen Ross Russell (Children's Press, 1970)

When Summer Ends by Susi Gregg Fowler (Greenwillow Books, 1989)